Quotable
EDDIE ROBINSON

Quotable
EDDIE ROBINSON

408 Memorable Quotes about Football,
Life, and Success by and about College Football's
All-time Winningest Coach

Aaron S. Lee

TowleHouse Publishing
Nashville, Tennessee

TowleHouse books are distributed by National Book Network (NBN),
4720 Boston Way, Lanham, Maryland 20706.

**A portion of the royalties from the sale of this book are being donated to the
Grambling University Athletic Foundation.**

Quotable Eddie Robinson is a compilation of brief quotes by and about Eddie
Robinson, excerpted from a variety of previously published works. This book was
not commissioned or authorized by Eddie Robinson.

Library of Congress Cataloging-in-Publication Data

Robinson, Eddie.
   Quotable Eddie Robinson : 408 memorable quotes about football, life, and suc-
cess by and about college football's all-time winningest coach / Aaron S. Lee.
      p. cm. -- (Potent quotables)
Includes bibliographical references.
   ISBN 1-931249-21-0
   1. Robinson, Eddie--Quotations. 2. Football coaches--United States--
Quotations. 3. Football--Coaching--Quotations, maxims, etc. I. Lee, Aaron Soon
Yong, 1972- II. Title. III. Series.
   GV939.R58 A35 2003
   796.332 '64--dc21

                                                               2002155290

Cover design by Gore Studio, Inc.
Page design by Mike Towle

Printed in the United States of America
1 2 3 4 5 6—07 06 05 04 03

CONTENTS

INTRODUCTION

L IKE THE TINA TURNER song says, Eddie Robinson was "Simply the best . . . better than all the rest."

The mark Eddie G. Robinson left on college football, and the sport in general, is unmistakable. It's hard to imagine that anyone will ever again serve as a head coach (at one university) for fifty-seven years, earn over four hundred coaching victories, or send as many players to the professional ranks as Coach Rob did during his tenure at Grambling State University.

By the time he retired in 1997, Robinson had a career coaching record of 408-165-15, with seventeen Southwestern Athletic Conference championships and nine National Black College titles. Not bad for the graduate of Louisiana's Leland College and someone who would move to the tiny North Louisiana town of Grambling, Louisiana, in 1942 to take over as head football coach at the age of twenty-two.

Coach Robinson was a motivator and teacher. Most important, he was a competitor, and that competitive nature rubbed off on his players. He wanted to be the best in whatever he did, whether it was coaching in a championship football game or playing jacks or tiddlywinks with the kids. He wanted to be the best in all of his endeavors, and he passed that same pride and work ethic on to his players.

He didn't only want to be the best in athletics or games. He wanted to be the best in everything. He is the type of person who wants to be the best student, the best teacher, the best worker, and the most liked. He always wanted to tell the best joke, too.

But even with all of that competitive drive, Coach Robinson wanted the best for his players as people as well as student-athletes. He stressed getting as much education as you could get and making the most of every opportunity you receive. He made sure his players were in church on Sundays and made sure they woke in time to attend class every morning.

Coach Robinson has always wanted to be the best American he can be. Realizing the results of hard work and dedication, he truly feels he is living "the American Dream" in the greatest country in the world. Eddie Robinson is thankful to live in a country like America, and America should be thankful to have produced a legend such as Eddie Robinson.

After everything he has seen and been through in his life, Coach Rob has a wealth of information he still passes on to younger generations. I'm thankful I was able to play for him at Grambling, because I know he played a big role in my athletic success both in college and in the pros. He taught me to be a player and a coach. He also helped teach me to be a man. I'm fortunate to have learned from one of the greatest teachers of all time.

Eddie Robinson touched the life of every football player he ever coached or coached against, and his words are tools that can continue teaching all people for generations to come. The world will be a better place for every person who reads and learns from the insight and words of wisdom Coach Rob passed along over the years.

—**Doug Williams**

ACKNOWLEDGMENTS

T O EDDIE ROBINSON, Scott Boatright, Glen Lewis, Doug
Williams, O. K. "Buddy" Davis, Steven Moody, Jeff Robertson,
Phil Latham, Jim Coleman, Travis Davis, and Mike Towle.
You gave . . . I achieved.

To R. J. Dykes, Peggy Kerr, R. P. Engle, Jim McCutchens,
Keats Mullikin, Bill Harper, Jeff Welch, and Bob Speights.
You gave . . . I grew.

To all my family and friends.
You gave . . . I appreciated.

To my parents, Ricky and Beth Lee.
You gave . . . and gave . . . and gave.

To my beautiful wife and best friend, Joanna.
You loved . . . and for us, this is only the beginning.

PREFACE

WHETHER THEIR world is one of politics, entertainment, or athletics, people from all walks of life have stepped to the plate during times of turmoil and triumph to deliver words of inspiration, hope, and courage. It is because of these great individuals that we—as ordinary people—find solace and leadership.

One of the greatest of these motivators is the winningest college football coach ever, Grambling State University's Eddie Robinson. Robinson's feat of 408 victories is surpassed only by the fact that he had one job and one wife throughout his life.

Without a doubt, Robinson's increasing international popularity transcends college football. He has dined with presidents, coached in the first college football games held outside the United States (Tokyo, 1976–1977), and was the first representative of a historically black football program to grace the cover of *Sports Illustrated*.

Quotable Eddie Robinson is just another example of Coach Robinson's achievements. His words are often as poetic as they are profound, as candid as they are sincere. He is a wordsmith with an effortless ability to create words of significance. He has always said what he feels and felt what he said. Coach Robinson may have stepped away from the sidelines, but he will never step out of our hearts.

Here's to you, Mr. Robinson.

FOREWORD

WHEN STATE FARM ENTERED a three-year title sponsorship with the Bayou Classic in 1996, the rivalry between Grambling State University and Southern University was already a storied tradition, and Eddie Robinson was already a legend. After meeting Coach Robinson for the first time, I realized what a special partnership this was going to be, and indeed has been for more than seven years.

At State Farm, we believe in the dreams and potential of young people, and we believe in the power of education to help them get there. We could not have selected a finer event than the Bayou Classic to represent what State Farm stands for, and I certainly cannot think of a better role model for our young people than Coach Robinson.

On behalf of State Farm Insurance Companies, it is my pleasure to recognize and thank Coach Robinson for his many outstanding accomplishments.

—*Chuck Wright*
Senior Vice President/Chief Agency and Marketing Officer
State Farm Insurance Companies

I.
The Game

The game of football has been played for more than one hundred years. It is a game of passion that is unequaled, a game of pageantry that is magnified, and a game of tradition that is timeless.

And perhaps no one person has ever summed up the game of football any better than coach Eddie Robinson did as the guest speaker of the Sixty-eighth Annual American Football Coaches Association convention held in New Orleans in December 1990.

His words, contained in the quote that immediately follows, define football as much as football has defined America.

1. Football builds character in boys. It makes them strong enough to know when they are weak and brave enough to face themselves when they are afraid. It will teach them to be proud and unbending in honest failure; but humble and gentle in success, not to substitute words for actions, nor to seek the path of comfort, but to face the stress and spur of difficulty and challenge.

2. It's a great game.

3. As much as you want it to be just another game, it's not.

4. When I was a kid they had those shows like *Alice in Wonderland* and *Make-Believe*, but in football, you just don't do that.

5. When you have played the game for as long as I have, three years in high school, four years in college, and played sandlot, it's been winning and losing all my life.

⁓

6. I used to draw plays in my notebooks and my teacher would kinda get on to me. She'd say, "Eddie, you can't be around football all your life."

⁓

7. When I was a kid in Baton Rouge, I would listen to the Sugar Bowl on a radio owned by this Italian fellow. I would have wanted to go, but I couldn't get in.

⁓

8. If you don't have a commitment, if you don't have a heart, you don't need to be in this game.

⁓

9. There is something in this game . . . it gives you something to live by.

⁓

10. It is always a challenge competing against the young guys.

⌒

11. I love this game, but I love the young men who play the game more than I love the game.

⌒

12. The game wouldn't be any good if it weren't for old-timers to sit around and tell about the good ol' days.

⌒

13. The media is the greatest thing to happen to athletes and their families because it gives them a way to always relive the great moments in their lives.

⌒

BAYOU CLASSIC

14. New Orleans is the city where Southern (University) and Grambling come each year for our last game on the last Saturday in November to decide, regardless of our record, whether it has been a winning season.

⌒

15. We've given NBC a great game. You don't have to have an interest in either school to get involved when you watch.

⌒

16. I dreamed and we broke some things down and we got into the same stadium where they played the Sugar Bowl and we drew seventy-six thousand paid for the largest crowd ever and I stood on the field and said, "We passed the hurdle." I couldn't come here as a player, but I brought my team in.

⌒

17. I wanted to play in New Orleans. This is Louisiana, where we're from, and I always felt we should play at least one of our biggest games here.

⌒

18. I remember standing on the sideline when all those people started coming in. I remember when they announced the attendance (76,753), I said, "What?" Nobody could believe it. Man, tears just started rolling down my face, and I started hugging people. They probably wondered what was wrong with me, but that was one of the highlights of my life.

⌒

19. I grow prouder of the Bayou Classic every day because it is the only national game that Louisiana's got.

HERITAGE BOWL

20. The Heritage Bowl can be a great thing for black college football.

GAME DAY

21. It's a new year with a new team, so anything can happen.

22. For some forty-seven years, I've been playing and having fun.

—*October 1989*

23. It's like going to a movie every day. You see new runners, new blockers, great runs, great plays, and great tackles.

The annual Bayou Classic was the source of some of Coach Robinson's greatest moments. (Grambling State University photo)

24.
I never get tired of the preparation part of the game.

25. I like to stand across the field from a guy and feel that, through other people, I can do some things.

26. I've learned that with every passing year, you have to be better prepared. A few years ago when we were struggling, I knew I had to work harder and put more into the game. I couldn't ask of others what I wouldn't be willing to do.

27. I am always concerned about our line play, because so much of a team's success either moving the football or stopping someone from scoring lies in those areas.

28. When I saw film on them, I could see their linebackers snortin' and rarin' to go.

    —on preparing for a game with Central State in 1987

29. It's been like watching a horror movie watching tapes of Bethune-Cookman, because they've got an outstanding passing attack.

30. (Bethune-Cookman's) offense is similar to the way (Bill) Walsh runs the show for the San Francisco 49ers. Sometimes you see them throwing even to the coaches on the sidelines.

31. Our players have not lost any confidence. We've got the talent and the players to win. We just have to start putting everything together. We need more intensity and aggressiveness on defense, and we need to get into the end zone more.

II.
The Job

Coaching was never a job for Eddie Robinson—it was a passion. He was hooked on the third grade after a local high school coach visited his school. He simply never wanted to do anything else. Robinson, whose career predated America's entry into World War II, has always approached the profession with determination and a grand sense of responsibility—responsibility to the school, the alumni, the coaching staff, and to the young men who played the game.

He was a student of the game and a proponent of the profession. Robinson's phenomenal coaching success may one day be duplicated, but his love for the trade will never be equaled.

32. The late Alonzo Stagg said it's the greatest profession in the world and it's the most rewarding profession in the world and that no man is too good to coach the American youth—I agree with him.

33. The way I used to coach has passed the boards.

34. I've never approached my job as running a football factory. I consider myself a teacher who tries to prepare athletes for life after their playing days are over.

35. A long time ago, I used to go and accept an award and I'd say, "Eddie, you're a helluva coach. Boy, you're really doing the job." But as I got older, I was accepting these things for the other people because they were making it all possible for me.

36. I want to coach as long as I can compete with the younger coaches and as long as I can be an asset to Grambling.

    —after winning No. 324
    (Grambling 27, Prairie View 7) to pass Bear Bryant

37. I've always wanted to mean something to somebody. And whatever it is I've done, I just hope it means something to the youth.

    —on breaking Bear Bryant's record of 323 career victories

38. When I took this job, nobody was jumping to get it. I didn't have anybody but myself.

39. I have ridden on the backs of athletes and assistant coaches all of my life. Whatever I might be or will be given credit for achieving, they must share in it.

One of Robinson's practices from the early years, stressing the fundamentals.
(Grambling State University photo)

40. I want young coaches to know that this is a tough profession, but it is the most rewarding profession in the world.

41. IT'S OFTEN SAID THAT A COACH IS MANY TIMES LIKE A SECOND FATHER TO AN ATHLETE, BUT I CAN TRULY SAY THAT APPLIES TO COACH ROBINSON.
   —*NFL Hall of Fame defensive lineman Buck Buchanan on Eddie Robinson*

42. Now people have offensive coordinators and defensive coordinators, and they stand back. But I can't do that. I have to keep my hand in it.

43. I still can get lost every day at 3:30 P.M. on this practice field. I still love it that much.

44. I survived because of the love in my gut.

45. If I were coming out today, I don't know that I would choose football. I might be like these guys today and choose some form of business where I can make more money. But money is not everything.

46. I love coaching. It's all I've ever done. It's all I know, and it has never been a job to me.

47. If I can continue to have good health, be alert, and coach against these young coaches, I'll continue to coach as long as I can.

48. I'm a realist. Preparation is most important.

49.
Coaching is just like a people profession.

~

50. HE NEVER APPEARED TO BE IN A HURRY AS HE SINGLED OUT
A PARTICULAR PHASE OF THE OFFENSE OR DEFENSE. YOU
WERE MADE TO UNDERSTAND WHY IT WAS IMPORTANT TO
HAND THE BALL OFF THIS WAY OR THAT WAY . . . AND THE
ADVANTAGE YOU WOULD HAVE ON YOUR OPPONENT IF YOUR
PLAY WAS FLAWLESS. I HOPE THAT I WAS HALF THE TEACHER
THAT COACH ROBINSON REPRESENTS.

—*Henry Crosby, former player and*
graduate of Grambling High and Grambling State

51. A coach is in a position to do a lot of good, and that's
the real importance of this work.

52. Too many coaches are afraid to share what they know
with their competitors. We will never get better unless
we share.

53. I've been paid to play. I pity the guy who has a job
that he doesn't enjoy doing.

54. I don't believe any guy living could even enjoy being called "Coach" as much as I do.

55. I guess when you've been doing something as long as I have, it just seems natural.

56. We need some good young coaches to step forward.

57. If I'm going to be the coach I want to do the coaching, not be some figurehead.

58. Preparation is key. I've been to enough coaching clinics to know that the best-prepared teams are the teams that win.

59. Balance is our key and intense practice provides our sharpness.

60. Coach a boy as if he were your own son.

THE NFL

61. No one made me an offer I couldn't refuse.

    —*on his never going to the NFL*

62. When I came here, blacks did not play in the NFL. And I looked at myself and said, "Eddie, what is wrong with you? If other coaches can coach players to play in the NFL, why can't you?"

HIS DESIRE TO COACH

63. I wanted to coach since I was in the third grade.

64. When I was three years old, I had it in my mind to do this for a living. When I got to high school, the love for the game and for the profession grew even more.

65. The teachers would get on to me about drawing football plays in my notebook.

66. My teachers used to tell me that I could not think about football all of the time and that I could not make a living being around a game.

67. I just knew there was a calling for me to be on the sidelines, helping some youngster become a better player and person.

68. As soon as I could spell *football*, I knew that I wanted to be a coach.

69. I liked to hang around the bench to see what the coach was doing.

COACHING

70. You, the coach, must create in your men a real love for the game and a spirit of work, determination, and loyalty.

71. The coach must be absolutely sincere in his work. He cannot win the confidence of his men unless he himself is in dead earnest. The coach must never give his men reason to doubt his integrity.

72. I believe that good coaches are teachers—including coordinators, offensive and defensive, and position coaches.

73. Each practice should be carefully planned in advance with room for modification.

74. A coach should know exactly what is to be done with each minute of time available. No coach should go onto the field without direction.

75. Head coaches must study their players and (coaches). This will enable them to understand their disposition and personalities.

76. Repetition in practice is a necessity. It is my job as a coach to continually drill for perfection of technique and for correct habit formation.

77. I just never got tired of being a coach. That's all I have ever wanted to do.

CHEATING

78. It does worry me to have the people of Louisiana and across the country where we play think that I would cheat to win. Hell . . . winning games just doesn't come to me like that.

79. Man, you know, cheating to win a game? I don't want anything to happen to me as Eddie Robinson. I don't need to do that.

80. I don't give a damn what nobody says. I know what I want my image to be. I don't have to steal. I don't have to lie.

81. I wouldn't know how to go and ask a teacher to change a grade. I have too much pride to do that.

III.
The Victories

If everyone likes a winner, then everyone must love Eddie Robinson, because all he has ever done his entire life is win.

Coach Robinson's 408 career coaching victories are tops in a world of college football that is filled with great teams led by even greater men.

He averaged a stunning seven and a half wins per season as he compiled forty-five winning seasons—twenty-seven consecutively—during his fifty-seven-year career. He never suffered back-to-back losing seasons during his first fifty-three years on the job. In fact, he only recorded three losing seasons during his first forty-five years at the helm of Grambling State.

Coach Robinson has won or shared in twenty-six college football championships or titles—including seventeen Southwestern Athletic Conference championships and nine

National Black College crowns. During one sixteen-year span (1966–1982), Robinson's Tigers won twelve SWAC championships.

In 1942, during Coach Robinson's second season, Grambling State finished with a flawless 9-0 record without getting scored on. The Tigers became only the second college team to accomplish such a feat and no team has—or probably will ever—do it again.

Due to World War II, the Tigers did not field a football team for two years (1943–1944), so Robinson coached the local Grambling High School team and successfully guided them to a state championship.

The little boy from Baton Rouge, Louisiana, grew up to become a man that would later become a legend—a legend who was nothing but a winner.

82.

Winning is not a sometimes thing. It is an all-the-time thing. There is no room for second or third place. It has always been American zeal to win and win and win. In order to win you've got to pay the price. It is not typical of Grambling not to pay the price.

83. Players must be confident about having a good season. That is a very important characteristic in having a successful year.

84. After a disastrous 1941 campaign, Grambling was unbeaten in 1942. Call it blind luck or fool's gold, we were still undefeated.

85. The greater will to win is often the deciding factor in a close game, and coaches must send their men into the game determined to win.

86. After the fundamentals are learned, it is morale that makes the team.

87. When I talk to them, you never tell them they can't accomplish anything. You tell them they have the ability but they aren't willing to pay the price.

88. My reputation helps, but you can't live on that.

89. The coaches laugh at me, but ever since we started winning, I had on at games the same shoes, same socks, the same pair of shorts, the same undershirt, the same deodorant, the same toilet water (cologne), the same shirt, the same pants, the same coat. I don't want to change my luck.

90. I want to be respected as one who can coach as well as anyone else, but most of all, I want this world to know that I passed this way, that I didn't cheat, and I tried to be fair with every boy that played for me.

91. Like any profession, you want to be the best. Life is a challenge.

⌒

92. I wouldn't hang around if I couldn't win.

⌒

93. You have to learn to win without bragging and lose without excuses.

⌒

94. The will to win, the desire to succeed, the urge to reach your full potential . . . these are the keys to unlock the door to personal excellence.

⌒

95. My advice to Doug (Williams) is simple. Great coaches surround themselves with great athletes. That's the main secret to winning.

⌒

96. The opportunity to go out a winner or loser would really more or less motivate you if you know that this is your last year.

97. Whatever league you're in, whatever level, win there.

98. (It is) winning and trying to make the young people realize the potential of what they can actually do and what's out there.

99. Well, last year's kisses don't excite us this year.

100. I don't want to overemphasize winning, but winning beats anything that comes in second.

101. If you don't want to win, there's no place in football for you.

102. All I want to do is just coach, compete, and try to win.

103. Win without braggin'. Lose without acting the fool.

104. There's no work too hard if it gets you what you need or where you want to go.

105. Hell, if you want to win, you've got to play to win. There ain't no messing around.

IV.
The Losses

Losing is not something the winningest college football coach
of all time knows a whole lot about. After all, Eddie Robinson
did not earn that distinction for finishing too many games with
the fewest points on the scoreboard. He is not a man who has
ever accepted losing. In fact, he simply has no tolerance for it.
According to Robinson, "There is no place for second or
third."

During his fifty-seven-year career, Robinson felt the sting
of only twelve losing seasons. Although his career ended after a
3-8 campaign, his legacy will forever live on as a man who loved
victory, but hated defeat even more.

106. I always blame Eddie Robinson. I try to figure out where I've failed them. I don't ever tear the ball club down. But we don't have excuses. Sometimes we just get whipped.

107. If you can't laugh at yourself, you're in trouble. We're in trouble right now, but I still plan to laugh.

108. If you lose, you want to lose to the best.

109. We knew all along that Central State had a good team. Now, everybody knows.

—after a loss

110. We dropped so many passes. We were within the other
      team's ten-, fifteen-yard-lines two, three, four times
      and didn't convert. You do that, you get whipped.

111. For about three years we lost our shirt at the
      Bayou Classic.

112. In 1987 we had our first losing season (5-6) in twenty-
      eight years. People were saying, "The game's passed
      him by." But the next season we went 8-3 and last
      year we won the conference.

113. Some writers were writing me off, but that is part of
      losing.

114. You know how guys do when you get to a certain age. They feel you ought to give it up.

115. I've worked hard at being a good coach. I've known the thrill of victory and the agony of defeat.

116. We have talent this year, but they have to produce and we have to coach them. I can't turn water into wine.

117. Either get a better player or get a player better.

118. I can't get used to people giving me all these tributes. They give me chairs, they give me presents, and then they come back and whip me. When you've been winning as long as we have, it's hard to get used to. We've lost to people who hadn't whipped me in twenty years.

    —on his final season at Grambling

119. When you lose, you hurt.

120. We'd dropped four games that first year, so I'd go in the back door of the dining hall, go into a supply room, and eat by myself.

121. I have feelings, but I'd rather say good things than bad things.

122. I just don't believe that Eddie Robinson did everything he could have done to win the game.

123. You're just never satisfied with yourself after a loss.

124. COMPETING AGAINST EDDIE ON A DAY LIKE TODAY . . . IT WOULD HAVE BEEN MUCH BETTER TO HAVE JUST BEEN A SPECTATOR.

    —*Bill Hayes, North Carolina A&T coach,*
    during Robinson's 37-35 loss at his home finale

125. I know you can't change things, but had we played like that in other games we would have a better record.

126. Walking out a winner would mean a lot to me, more than walking out on your worst season.

127. You certainly don't want to go out the last season of your career like this one.

128. To walk out with seven whippings this year and not have the chance to pay those guys back, no way.

129. I'm still hurting over this season and all the things that have been happening.

130. That's something I never worry about, maybe they had something else to do.

    —*on poor crowd attendance at his final home game*

131. This is the worst year I've ever had. I can't sleep. I never thought it would be possible for me to lose eight games in a season. Maybe I don't have the drive anymore, but I just can't get it in my head that I can't win.
     —*on his final year*

132. If I'd known what this year was going to be like, I'd probably have quit last year.

133. I'm fighting for survival. I'm fighting to lead the Black and Gold again.

134. I know I can't stay here forever and keep losing, but I thought they would tell me I'd have one more year before I had to go.

135. I'm concerned about how we played today. We were hopeful of being better prepared, but we weren't. Maybe we were out-coached. If that's so, it has happened that way for the last three years.
     —*after a third straight loss to Southern*

136. Maybe the game has passed me by. I don't know. Even though I have real good coaches, I need to spend more time with my team.

137. I have so many commitments away from the football field and that worries me. I think I might have over-committed myself for the recruiting season, too.

138. I told my team they weren't cheated out there today. The officials were good. I told them if they wanted to blame anybody, don't blame the officials. I told them to start with me.

139. I lost eight games and I lost the Bayou Classic. And if I said that doesn't hurt, then I'd be lying.

The look is mod with his squad, the expression intense.
(Grambling State University photo)

140.
The kids cried, but in their heart I know they under-stood me and were with me.

—after losing a game, 9-7, on the final play, going for the touchdown at the one-foot line instead of kicking a field goal

V.
The Record

When the Grambling State Tigers defeated Southwestern Athletic Conference rival Prairie View A&M 27-7 on October 5, 1985, at the Cotton Bowl in Dallas, Robinson had won his 324th career victory to surpass legendary coach Paul "Bear" Bryant as college football's all-time winningest coach.

Robinson had already become accustomed to breaking records and passing legends. A year earlier, he surpassed Glen "Pop" Warner with win No. 314, and then a week later he surpassed Amos Alonzo Stagg (315).

Now, both Penn State's Joe Paterno and Florida State's Bobby Bowden have surpassed Bryant's 323-victory mark and taken aim at Robinson's total, but neither Paterno nor Bowden—who are both in the twilight of their careers—will

*ever catch Robinson's mountainous 408. Only head coach
John Gagliardi, who began his fifty-fourth season in 2002 at
St. John's in Collegeville, Minnesota, has a realistic chance of
catching Robinson. But even with 388 career victories entering
the 2002 season, the seventy-five-year-old Division III coach
was still facing a daunting task.*

*Many have argued that Robinson never contended with
the caliber of competition that Bryant, Paterno, or Bowden
faced. But according to Robinson, "A win is a win, no matter
what." He always claimed that he played who he was told to
play and that was all he could do.*

*As further validation of his record, Robinson's 323rd
victory to tie Bryant was a 23-6 victory over Oregon State, a
Division I-A and Pac-10 school. The fact still remains that in
the world of college football coaching victories, Robinson is
king.*

141. If the "Bear" were still alive, I'd still be chasing him. I'm no better than any other coach. But I've heard the best coaches in America and learned from them for over sixty years.

142. The real record I have set for over fifty years is the fact that I have had one job and one wife.

143. YES, BEFORE HE ECLIPSED BEAR BRYANT'S RECORD FOR MOST VICTORIES, BEFORE MANY OF THE HALL OF FAME HONORS STARTED BEING BESTOWED UPON HIM, HE HAD ALREADY BECOME AN ICON, A ROLE MODEL, AND AN AMERICAN LEGEND.
    —*James Frank, Southwestern Athletic Conference commissioner, after Robinson's retirement*

144. I still don't know what this (setting a new record) means. Maybe one day I'll wake up and realize what I've done.

145.

I'm not concerned about personal records. Time takes care of everything and it will eventually take care of that. All it means is that I've been around for a long time.

146. I haven't blocked or tackled anybody. I have just tried
to give encouragement to the young men who have
played for Grambling. The record belongs to everybody, all the former players, all the assistant coaches,
and all the loyal fans who have supported Grambling
throughout the years. Eddie Robinson sure hasn't
done it all.

147. I'm so busy trying to get ready for the next game that I
haven't decided what it really means.

—on becoming the winningest coach of all time

148. You see what the other guys like (Amos Alonzo) Stagg
and (Pop) Warner and Coach (Paul) Bryant and all
these other guys had a chance to see.

—his vantage point given his success at Grambling

149. I could always see myself as a good coach, possibly as
one of the best coaches. But nobody knew it because I
was dreaming.

150. I dreamed what it would be like winning all those games like Coach Bryant did, more than anyone else. And it happened.

151. Everything has to come to an end. But it wouldn't be like I wanted to win four hundred games. It is just a number.

152. Ever since Coach Bryant died, (the record) hasn't meant as much. I can't call and talk to him about it.

153. I would get out at 398, but I have this agreement with the school to stay until four hundred. But it might be better to get out now and get another job.

154. Every once in a while someone asks, "Don't you get tired?" And I say, "No, no, no!"

155. Without my assistant coaches, without the support of my family, and without the contributions of so many fine players and young men, none of this would be possible.

156. IT COULDN'T HAVE HAPPENED TO A BETTER MAN. I JUST WISH IT WOULD HAVE HAPPENED A WEEK LATER.
    —*Conway Hayman, former Prairie View coach, on Robinson's 324th victory over his Panthers*

157. In 1977, Dr. Jones told me this could be happening.
    —*referring to Dr. Ralph Waldo Emerson Jones, former Grambling president*

158. I'd be the only guy with a halfway chance to catch him, and I'm not going to do it.
    —*John Gagliardi, Division III coach at St. John's, after winning No. 270*

159. NO DIVISION I COACH IS GOING TO CATCH HIM. THEY'D HAVE TO WIN TEN GAMES A YEAR FOR FORTY YEARS.

—Gagliardi

160. I have never thought about the records. I've just thought about the kids.

161. I guess it won't sink in until I'm out of coaching. I don't have time to sit and think about it.

162. I guess when you've been in this profession as long as I have, there are all kinds of numbers coming up.

—on his five hundredth career college football game

163. I want to give the fruits of the 408 wins to all the student-athletes and assistant coaches I have had. They are the ones who truly deserve the credit.

Almost everywhere Coach Robinson has gone, he has been surrounded by admirers. (Grambling State University photo)

164. People can do what they want with their record. They can put an asterisk on it if they want. That's their business.

165. EVERYBODY TALKS ABOUT THE RACE BETWEEN ME AND JOE (PATERNO). WELL, WHOEVER WINS IT NEEDS ONE HUNDRED MORE.

    —*Bobby Bowden, Florida State coach, referring to Robinson's 408*

166. If it had to happen, I'm just glad it happened in Louisiana. Happened at a Louisiana school. Happened to a person born in Louisiana and hadn't gone out of Louisiana until I got connected with football.

    —*on his four hundredth victory*

167. COACH ROBINSON'S LEGACY IS THAT HE IS THE WINNINGEST COLLEGE COACH IN AMERICA.

    —*James Carson, former Jackson State University head coach*

168. Sure it's great to win four hundred games, but I'd rather have winning seasons and not worry so much about big numbers like three hundred or four hundred.

⌒

169. I've tried to think this through and I haven't come up with why all of this has happened to me in my lifetime. I'm just at a loss for words.

⌒

170. The Hall of Fame, as the world knows, is the elite circle where many of the truly great contributors to the game of football are enshrined. I am thankful and very, very proud that you have chosen me on my merits and my career as a coach ranking with the truly immortals of the game.

⌒

ON PAUL "BEAR" BRYANT

171. He influenced everyone and was an inspiration.

⌒

172. He was a superstar and the first guy who let us know that it wasn't impossible to beat Alonzo Stagg's record of 314 wins.

173. We had hoped we would eventually get a chance to play (at Legion Field). Someone said, "He (Bryant) might have whipped you." But he whipped everybody else.

174. We always agreed to beat each other on the field and help each other off the field.

175. I'm sure if Coach Bryant was coaching today, he'd still be ahead of me in victories.

176. He was one of the most competitive men I have ever seen.

177. I've had men come to me and profess love for this man, love that brings them to tears. When you see this kind of thing, you wonder what you have to do to achieve that.

178. I realize the tremendous impact he has made on this sport. He's been a winner all his life.

ON AMOS ALONZO STAGG (who had 300 career victories)

179. Nobody thought Stagg's record would ever be broken.

180. I thought anyone that famous had to have three ears and two noses, so I wanted to get a closer look.

181. I shook his hand so long that someone behind me said, "All right, kiss him and move on."

A youthful Eddie Robinson would grow old gracefully as he went on to spend more than half a century coaching football at Grambling State. (Grambling State University photo)

VI.
The School

Coach Robinson spent his entire career at Grambling State University and he put the school on the map.

He began at age twenty-two after graduating in 1941 from the now-defunct Leland College in Baker, Louisiana, just outside of the state capital, Baton Rouge.

Coach Robinson's monthly salary was a mere $63.75 compensation for a job that initially included coaching the football, basketball, and baseball teams, heading the athletics department, and handling groundskeeping duties. How many other college football coaching legends had to cut the grass on their own football fields?

But Robinson's love affair with the university flourished, and as much as he believed in the success of Grambling State, he believed in education even more.

57

Neither of Robinson's parents finished high school, but both understood the importance of an education. They encouraged a young Eddie to stay in school and receive a college degree.

Besides earning a bachelor of arts degree from Leland, Robinson also earned a master's degree from the University of Iowa in 1954. Robinson has also been awarded honorary doctorate degrees from Louisiana Tech University, Southern University, Yale University, and Grambling State.

Robinson's fulfillment in life came from not only his coaching success but also his success as a pioneer and ambassador for education at Grambling State.

182. My state (Louisiana) dictates to me (through racial segregation) where I'd go to school and when I got out, where I could coach and the schedule I could play.

—on Grambling being in the NCAA's Division I-AA instead of I-A

GRAMBLING STATE UNIVERSITY

183. Years ago we didn't have a monopoly because we had to recruit against other black schools to get the great players. Certainly, it doesn't come as easy as it once did. But this is the way it's supposed to be. You don't get anything handed to you because you're black. We graduate more football players than most schools.

184. We know our strengths and weaknesses, and we emphasize the positive things that we have to offer. And that starts with education. We don't downgrade other schools. We emphasize the percentage of athletes we graduate, that they do graduate and work in the profession of their choice, and yes, a pro football career is available for those who work hard and achieve.

185. Grambling has been known for decades as the place "Where Everybody is Somebody," and that includes our athletes.

186. All I've ever known was Grambling. I wasn't going to change schools. When you leave, you limit what you can accomplish.

187. I think what has happened in our life at Grambling is important because of what it has made us become.

188. If I couldn't compete with the young coaches and if I were not a plus for the university, I'd get out of here tomorrow.

189. When I was at Grambling, I wanted to know how I could change things.

190. I REMEMBER WHEN WE FIRST WENT OVER TO THE NEW STADIUM, COACH ROBINSON CRIED. HE DIDN'T THINK HE'D EVER GET IT.

—Dr. Joseph B. Johnson, former Grambling president

191. That was hard to get over . . . a stadium being named after you, and now this. Sometimes you just need to sit down and count your blessing.

—on being honored with a grant for an Eddie Robinson museum

192. Unless Grambling sends me away, I'm going to try to beat somebody, and I'm going to get some football players. I want to come back there.

193. It almost comes close to what Dr. Martin Luther King said about having gone to the top of the mountain.

—on his success at Grambling

194. I do believe football has made a contribution to the well-being of Grambling and to the growth of Grambling.

195. Playing in New York, playing in Tokyo, playing on the West Coast, playing on the eastern seaboard, and this type of thing, it's had a lot to do with the enrollment.

196. A car wash is a big fund-raiser for us. But, seriously, we know we don't have the financial capabilities of many, many other schools around the nation.

197. The numbers aren't there for us in the alumni groups. But the people we have are very supportive and do a great service to the university by the way they come out and support the players and coaches.

198. I want them to leave Grambling with the sense that they can make it in this world.

199. I love Grambling, I love Ruston and northern Louisiana. If you're accustomed to that, you don't just give it up.

200.

Grambling is my home, the people here are all my friends. It's like one big, happy family.

201. They built this stadium and they named it after me, but they didn't have the money to finish it. So, I told them to forget about the dressing rooms, we would use the ones we had across campus and walk to the field. And now they have the money, and they are going to build us a nice dressing room. It all works out.

202. We walk over here by the girls' dorm every day. The players want to strut by with their uniforms on. They probably would talk about firing me if I took that away from them. So we walk.

203. I think it's situations like this where it pays off to try to live right, to be loyal, and just try to do the best job you can.

204. Well, if I feel as if I can still compete and make a contribution, then I want an opportunity to show that I can do it. I want that opportunity because I love Grambling, and Grambling has been good to me.

205. IF ANYONE CAN BE IDENTIFIED WITH GRAMBLING ATHLETICS, IT'S EDDIE ROBINSON. HE LITERALLY PUT THE SCHOOL ON THE MAP. PEOPLE KNOW ABOUT GRAMBLING BECAUSE OF HIM.
     —*John Rawlings*, The Sporting News

206. They changed the name of the school to Grambling University. Used to be when the other team was down at our goal line, our students would yell, "Hold the line, Louisiana Negro Normal and Industrial Institute!" Before they could finish the cheer, the other guys would score.

207. You know, when they call the roll, I would like to feel I have made some positive contribution to society, some little something. Coaching for coaching's sake is fine, but there are other things—like teaching boys to compete in society—and I don't know if I could have done some things I've done anywhere else than Grambling.

EDUCATION

208. If I had been a science teacher, I would have wanted to send my students to NASA to see someone among them go into space. But I'm in football, so what I want first is to see them graduate—that degree is really what will be most important to them—and second to play in the NFL.

209. I'm concerned about what kind of person a student will be when he leaves college.

210. Everybody can't become a professional football player. Everybody is not cut out to be a professional athlete. Even more important to our society are the young people who go on to become doctors, lawyers, and educators. It pleases me to know that we've had our share of athletes from Grambling who have become a success in those fields, too.

211. I just want everybody here to know how thankful I am
      for having coached so many fine young men who
      chose Grambling for their college education.

212. Whether they're going to graduate, that's what I'm
      concerned about.

213. If he (a player) comes here and plays for us and he
      leaves with a degree or gets near it so he can stay
      another year, he is a winner.

214. People could never realize the joy it is to sit at
      commencement and see these guys walk across the
      stage and graduate. You've seen them play, you know
      from whence they come, and you see them go, and
      you see them with a degree.

215. Frankly, a degree means a lot of money for a person in a lifetime and it represents a lot of service that this person can give back to his city, his country, and this kind of thing and make a good living.

216. A LOT OF COACHES JUST TALKED ABOUT IT, BUT COACH ROBINSON SEES THAT YOU GET TO THE STUDY HALL. HE KEEPS A SCHEDULE OF EVERYBODY'S CLASSES AND IF YOU'RE NOT THERE, HE COMES AFTER YOU.
—*Doug Williams, former Grambling quarterback*

217. You don't major in football. You play the game.

218. I never considered myself an unusual teacher during all these years. I do know that I had to convince hundreds of young black men that they could be as good as anyone else, on and off the football field.

219. It never occurred to me that they would fail at anything they were doing as athletes. Nor did it ever cross my mind that each player would not be a better person after our athletic experiences together. I don't see how a teacher can feel any other way.

⌒

220. I would hope that my teaching went beyond the scope of football.

⌒

ON FORMER GRAMBLING STATE PRESIDENT DR. RALPH WALDO EMERSON JONES

221. Dr. Jones said he was the best pitcher these parts had ever seen. I said I could hit any pitcher I faced. He said, "Let's get a mitt and we'll see." We went outside. His brief warmup told me the man could throw. But I could hit. Suddenly, I remembered it was a job I was after. I went down swinging on three straight pitches—and I got the job.

—on his hiring at Grambling

⌒

222. Dr. Jones, a charismatic individual, dreamed of making Grambling the black Notre Dame. He persisted in launching the most ambitious athletic program yet produced by a minority institution that confined black colleges to a marginal world.

223. For fifty years he symbolized Grambling as an astute, capable, responsible, dedicated educator beyond compare.

224. He was the magnetic spark for Grambling's national mystique.

225. It has been my privilege to follow Dr. Jones's footsteps by serving Grambling for one-half century.

VII.
The Players

During his fifty-seven-year career at Grambling, Coach Robinson sent more than two hundred players to the National Football League, more than any other college football coach in the country. Robinson coached eighty-five All-Americans and had seven players selected in the first round of the NFL draft.

Former players such as Willie Davis, Willie Brown, Junious "Buck" Buchanan, and Charlie Joiner have gone on to earn professional football's crowning achievement, enshrinement into the NFL's Hall of Fame.

Current Grambling State head football coach and former All-American quarterback Doug Williams achieved great success on the field with a four-touchdown performance in Super Bowl XXII and was named the game's Most Valuable Player as the Washington Redskins defeated the Denver Broncos in one of the more memorable Super Bowls.

Coach Robinson has always shared a special relationship with every player who participated in the Tigers' football program, and he took pride in graduating close to 80 percent of his athletes. He seemed to take extra satisfaction in players who became doctors, lawyers, or educators. He treated "every player like his own son" and he believed that "You coach 'em as though he were the boy you want to marry your daughter."

To many, he was a strict disciplinarian and brilliant strategist, but to all he was a loveable father figure who only wanted the best for every young man who played for him.

226. Leadership, like coaching, is fighting for the hearts and souls of men, to get them to believe in you.

227. We call it payback, our ex-players returning to the campus to assist with spring practice or to talk to the players.

228. To have a good team, you must first have good players.

229. A coach must know or learn that no two players are exactly alike.

230. The coach must know each individual player as a person.

231. They want discipline, they still do.

Manning the blocking sled while two of his players drive him back.
(Grambling State University photo)

232. If you want to continue coaching, the big thing is, you can't forget what you did at seventeen, eighteen, nineteen, or you can't handle the players.

233. Sometimes you just have to tell them you love them. That never changes.

234. I believe I know everyone's name on the team now. But back then, I knew all their names and all the names of their mamas and daddies, too.

235. I've had to change. They try to get out of stuff more than ever before, but I just try to remain fair. If you do something for one, you have to be prepared to do it for seventy others. There is no star system.

236. I am not trying to be a bully, but you will run those damn bleachers and do what you are supposed to do.

237. The guy you think doesn't have it might just be the one to pick up the ball and run with it.

238. You can't jive them, you have to be yourself. And you have to earn their respect. If he is a man, treat him like one.

239. I want my players to always see me in church.

240. We travel to all these nice places and stay in nice hotels, and we wear coats and ties because we ain't going to no beach.

241. We have a course (at Grambling) called Everyday Living. It teaches them social graces, so when a guy goes out to eat, he knows what piece of silver to pick up and about opening doors. You know how many people turn down dinner invitations because they don't know how to eat?

242. It can't be all serious; you have to have some fun and laugh with them.

243. They agitate you so much that you have to have some things so they think that you're crazy.

244. I got a pair of earrings in my pocket, in this envelope, that I collected from a player yesterday. If you wear it and I see it, it belongs to me.

245. (The players) have these (pictures of) nude women on the walls of their room. I told them to cover up the vital parts or I was going to invite their mamas to come to their rooms and see what you have up and tell me it is okay.

246. One time (the players) were acting silly, and I couldn't get them to pay attention. So I wrote their mamas and had them come to practice on a Friday. They started to pull up in their big cars, and man, you should have seen those players. They straightened out right quick.

247. When they come out of Grambling, they have my signature on them.

248. They aren't the English teacher's kids or the math teacher's kids, they are Eddie's boys, and I try to make them better than average.

249. You get a piece of every kid that plays for you, and he should take a piece of you.

250. You have to love the kids to coach them. If you don't, you won't be able to do the type of job that is necessary.

251. You have to go out and find the players, but they have to be good people.

252. The football players are the most important people to me. I like being around them. I like teaching and seeing them succeed in life. That gives me the greatest thrill.

253. (The players) forget that I've got a key to every room in the athletic dormitory.

254. The player is the most important part of the game.

255. I talk about being a good person to our team and things like that. I want them to be good men.

256. I try to coach them as though every one of those players was my son. Deep down, I just want them to be the best.

257. When a man loses his pride, he isn't worth a damn.

258. I haven't given very much thought to my players being any different today in the nineties than they were in the sixties.

259.

I like to see my players come to me as boys and leave us as men.

260. I have to deal with every problem that my players face. Their problems are my problems. It's all in a day of teaching and coaching.

261. Coaches should build men first and football players second.

262. I don't have uniforms that fit men under 250 pounds.

263. I never won a single game in my life. The players did.

264. I do not consider myself a great coach, I just think that the good Lord decided to let Eddie Robinson have some good football players.

DRUGS

265. I try to be fair with them. I tell them what I think it takes to live in America. I tell a player if he's going to mess around with those damn drugs, he can't play on this team.

266. I explain (to players) that when you use drugs, you lose your sex drive. You should see how big their eyes get.

ON DOUG WILLIAMS

On his most rewarding moment as a coach:

267. When Doug Williams, the former Grambling quarterback, got up off the ground to lead the Washington Redskins to the Super Bowl championship in 1988. He not only exhibited outstanding ability in that game, but also determination, resiliency, and self-confidence—all the qualities you look for in leaders.

268. That was the first time that I challenged the deity. Well, not challenged. But when Doug went down, I pointed up and said, "I know you didn't bring me out here for this."

    —*referring to Super Bowl XXII*

269. We must admit it is a great feeling to have had the first black quarterback to start in the NFL and the first to start and win a Super Bowl in James Harris and Doug Williams (respectively) from our school. The same is true about having the three persons enshrined into the NFL Hall of Fame.

270. I'm not concerned about Doug. We (Grambling) got the coach we want and he'll do a good job. Now I'm concerned about getting the fans fired up so they pack the stadium for home games and support Doug.

271. Doug Williams is simply awesome.

272. I'm talking about great players. And when you talk about those players, Doug Williams has to be one of those at the top of the list.

ON PAUL "TANK" YOUNGER

273. Tank was always special.

274. I told him he had to do more. I told him he'd have to be willing to push a little harder to make his mark, and what a mark he ended up making.

275. Younger was the first of an imposing list of All-Americans and All-Pro superstars developed at Grambling.

276. He pioneered the beginning of black stars into the NFL domain as a Los Angeles Rams discovery.

277. Following Younger's success as a college and pro star, a new spirit was evoked at Grambling.

ON EVERSON WALLS

278. Everson Walls was a natural talent, but he worked as hard as anybody else every single day.

ON ERNIE LADD

279. Ernie Ladd was one of the most intimidating football players to ever play the game.

ON CHARLIE JOINER

280. He had the best pair of hands and ran the prettiest routes of anybody I had ever seen.

ON WILLIE DAVIS

281. "Tank" observed Willie Davis and told me that he was going to be a great professional athlete—he was right.

ON JUNIOUS "BUCK" BUCHANAN

282. Buck has always been one of the most successful people both on and off the field. It just goes to show you how hard work really does pay off.

ON WILLIE BROWN

283. Willie Brown was always an excellent player and student of the game. He is doing a great job as an assistant coach on the collegiate level.

VIII.
The Family

It has often been said that Coach Robinson's proudest accomplishment was that he had one wife and one job for more than fifty years.

Eddie Robinson met Doris Mott in south Louisiana when they were in the seventh grade. The eight-year courtship ended when the two married on June 24, 1941.

Doris Robinson became the solid foundation that Coach Robinson depended on and found comfort in.

The Robinsons were blessed with two children, Lillian Rose Broaden and Eddie Robinson Jr.; five grandchildren, Cheryl Clifton, Sharon Moore, Eddie Robinson III, Michael Watkins, and Cherie Kirkland; nine great-grandchildren, Quentin Burrell, Brandon West, Sean Moore, Brittni

Watkins, Michael Watkins II, Channing Kirkland, Eddie Robinson IV, Chloe Robinson, and Jalen Clifton.

For Coach Robinson these names represent his most beloved possession—his family.

284. She is the best thing that has ever happened to me because she puts up with my crazy schedule and demands. She understands the unusual demands of this profession. But because she understands, it makes my job easier.

—on Doris

285. I think my job is next to my family.

286. We're ready for it but we kind of think and talk about the fact that you have to plan retirement like you plan other things, like game plans. My wife and I planned long ago for retirement.

—on retirement with Doris

287. If we, as adults, want to make sure our young people do the right things, then we've got to set an example.

288. One time in practice, my son Eddie (Jr.) got his nose smashed and knocked over to the side, and I told them to call the trainer and he took him away in a car. Ernie Ladd later told me that the players saw that I didn't go over there and wipe his face, that I didn't treat him differently than anyone else, and it was the talk of the dormitory.

⌒

289. It's like the car I drive, the back window is knocked out, but it gets me where I need to go. I don't need a car up in the house with me, sleeping in the next damn room.

⌒

290. Eddie Robinson needs a Cadillac? Hell, I can't worry about these things. I'm trying to win the next game.

⌒

291. I answer all the mail. It may take a while, but sooner or later I get them all done.

⌒

"Eddie Robinson needs a Cadillac. Hell, I can't worry about these things. I'm trying to win the next game." (Grambling State University photo)

292. Money is no big deal. I've never even had a contract (at Grambling). What I valued most is my family and what I got from my momma and daddy.

HIS HEALTH

293. I go to the doctor to keep from having to go to the doctor.

294. If I get a headache or any type of pain, I go to the doctor. They have always taken care of me.

295. High blood pressure? I don't have any high blood pressure. I take medicine for it and never have any problems with it.

ON DORIS

296. We started dating around the end of elementary school, so she's always been there for me. She's an important part of my foundation.

297. My wife complains that I don't make enough money.

298. I told my wife that Douglas MacArthur said, "Old soldiers never die, they just fade away." She told me that MacArthur didn't know that old coaches never go away, they just talk too long.

299. Honey, I'm the coach again.

—on being granted one more season to coach

300. My wife is as excited as hell when I come into the house because she says, "You're always gone . . . "

DORIS ON EDDIE

301. I'M A WIDOW DURING FOOTBALL SEASON.

302. I NEVER SEE EDDIE ONCE THE SEASON BEGINS.

303. HE'S ALWAYS BEEN A PERSON FOR WORK AND FOR TRYING TO
      SATISFY EVERYONE.

304. HE'S THE LIFE OF THE PARTY AND HE DOESN'T DRINK OR
      SMOKE.

305. I HAVE BEEN MARRIED TO EDDIE ROBINSON LONG ENOUGH
      NOT TO BE SURPRISED.

HIS CHILDHOOD

306. I guess Joe Louis had a greater impact on me than any
     other sports figure or anybody else other than my
     father. He never bragged, he never made a lot of
     promises and things like that, and I could relate to
     somebody like that.

     —on role models

307. What I've become I credit to my life on the farm.

308. (The farm) taught me the value of hard work, how to
     accept and overcome adversity, pride in a job well
     done. They are lessons that I've never forgotten and
     always use.

309. (Farm boys) are all alike—tenacious and disciplined.

310. I was one tough cotton picker.

311. We sneaked one time too many and my dad got on to me pretty good. He said if I was going to go to these football games, I'd better learn to pay to get in.

~

312. My daddy had the quickest belt in Baton Rouge.

~

313. (My daddy) didn't just whip you, he'd talk to you.
     He'd say, "I want you to be a good person." And then *whoop*!
     "You can grow up and do things on the street and they will put you in prison." And there'd be another *whoop*!
     And I'd say, "Well, just go ahead and whip me and don't talk to me."
     And he'd say, "Nooo."
     And he'd whip a while and talk a while.

~

314. My parents gave me a sense of pride and direction in life.

~

IX.
The Country

No one has ever been prouder to be an American than Eddie Robinson. Spend a minute with Coach Robinson and you will see that his patriotism is infectious and exhilarating. This from an African-American man who grew up during turbulent times filled with escalating racial tensions.

Coach Robinson has never made excuses or allowed any societal obstacles to become a crutch. Simply put, he is an American who has made the most of every opportunity and he has always been willing to declare it.

315.

America offers more opportunities to young people than any other country in the world. But opportunity comes at a price. You have to be prepared. If opportunity comes and you're not prepared, you can't have it. That's the bottom line.

316. I know anything is possible here in America.

317. I was never carried away by simply winning football games. I was carried away by the idea of building better Americans.

318. I knew that I could walk away from football. But I also knew that I could never walk away from our young people.

319. Our youth are our most precious possession.

320. We're losing the battle. Sometimes I wonder if it's something designed by another nation. Something is wrong, so frightening. Things are going down the drain. I don't believe a nation with our resources is really fighting the battle. We used to always rise to the occasion.

    —*on the U.S. drug problem*

321. The important thing is to fit in as a good American.

322. This is a great country. If you are willing to pay the price, you can be anything you want here, even if it comes slow sometimes.

323. I want my players to realize that after they play football, whether they go on to play for the NFL or not, they have to live in a very competitive society in this country.

324. I don't believe anybody can out-American me. I'm proud to be an American. I know I sometimes sound like a politician at a Fourth of July picnic, but I feel I am telling the truth when I tell people that we are living in the greatest country in the world.

325. Football, the athletes, and spectators have been good to me, and I don't have enough years left to pay them back. I try every day to pay them back in some form.

326. As long as I have my faculties, I'll do the right thing, because I wouldn't want to do anything that's not in the best interest of football nor anything that wouldn't stand for what's best in America.

327. There is a constitution, and you learn to work within the system.

328. I actually believe, and I could be wrong, that football—and athletics in general—has made this nation the best fighting team in the world.

329. If I ever doubted this was the greatest country in the world, I don't know.

330. If you try and dream, dreams can come true.

331. There's no finer place in the world to live than North Louisiana.

332. The only thing wrong with people is that if they're a
      senior citizen and they're ready for the chair in front of
      the television set, they think everybody else is ready for
      the chair.

      —on retirement

333. I learned very early on that despite a lot of obstacles,
      America gives you opportunity. And maybe that's the
      most important thing I can impress on my players.

334. I'm old-fashioned. To me there's still a right way and a
      wrong way.

335. That's the thing about sports. Once people can play
      together, they see they can live together.

336. I can't change what happened on September 11, but I
      can continue to support my country, the administra-
      tion, and be the best American I can be.

337. The key to the American dream is hard work.

338. In athletics we always say the way you play the game is the way you'll live your life.

RACE

339. If you've never been a minority, it's hard to understand the feeling that you are not quite an American. You find peace with yourself on that day when you decide, "I'm as much an American as anyone else."

340. I worked hard to be an American coach and not just a black coach.

341. The thing I stressed most often was how they, as blacks, had to love America as much as anybody else loved it.

342. You know, I stopped being a black coach a long time ago. I am an American coach, and I try to do what every American coach tries to do. I want to win, make my boys better men, and pass on those things that our society holds dearest.

343. I grew up in the South. I was told where to attend elementary school, where to attend high school. When I became a coach, I was told who to recruit, who I could play. I did what I could within the system.

344. All I want is for my story to be an American story, not black and not white. Just American. I want it to belong to everybody.

345. I dream there will be a black president of the United States, and I got to believe it will happen.

346. If you think you have two strikes on you because you're black and you aren't allowed to do anything, then you'll strike out.

X.
The End

*Every era must come to an end. Eddie Robinson's was no dif-
ferent. In 1996, the hottest topic in Louisiana was the future
of Eddie Robinson. Whether he should or shouldn't retire
sparked debate at every water cooler in the state. Eventually,
Louisiana governor Mike Foster intervened and helped secure
Robinson another season—a victory lap so to speak.*

*However, Robinson's "Farewell Tour" in 1997 was
greeted with few parades and even fewer packed stadiums.
Even his own Grambling State showed little interest as
Robinson coached his final home game in front of a
generously estimated crowd of forty-five hundred spectators in
a stadium that seats twenty thousand.*

*Some claimed the coach stayed too long and that the
game had passed him by . . . but Eddie Robinson remained*

diligent and steadfast that he wanted nothing more for Grambling than one more winning season. Although one last winning season never came and there was little fanfare to mark the end, the sheer magnitude of Robinson's historic career will forever remain untarnished and his accomplishments will live on in the record books forever.

347. It's no big deal that the alumni and people want me to leave football. And it's no big deal that I want to coach another year and then I want to come out of football, win or lose. But if I have a chance to have a winning season, I would like to come out a winner.

348. THE GOVERNOR PERSONALLY BELIEVES COACH ROBINSON HAS MEANT SO MUCH TO GRAMBLING, TO LOUISIANA, AND TO AMERICAN FOOTBALL—NOT JUST AS A COACH, BUT AS A LEADER OF YOUNG MEN—THAT HE (GOVERNOR FOSTER) WOULD LIKE FOR HIM (ROBINSON) TO HAVE A FAREWELL YEAR.
   —*Steve Perry, Louisiana chief of staff for governor Mike Foster*

349. I've been considering retirement for the past twenty-five years.

350. I've got fifty-five years here, and they've earned me the right to say when I'll retire.

351. And that's all I have wanted through all of this, just to have one last opportunity to have Grambling football on the winning side of the column again. After that, well, then they can do what they want to do.

352. I'M WEARY, IT'S BEEN TOO EVENTFUL THIS PAST YEAR, TOO MANY THINGS TO DO, TOO MANY PLACES TO GO, TOO MANY LATE HOURS AND LONG DAYS.

—Doris, upon her husband's retirement

353. BETWEEN ALL THE AWARDS, THE HOUSE IS EVEN MORE STUFFED WITH PLAQUES AND PICTURES, HE'S BEEN INTER-VIEWED AND I'VE BEEN INTERVIEWED. I'VE DRAGGED OUT PICTURES AND TOLD PEOPLE WHAT THEY ARE. THE PHONE HASN'T STOPPED RINGING.

—Doris

354. I DON'T KNOW WHAT HE'S GOING TO DO AFTER THAT. BUT KNOWING EDDIE, WE WON'T BE SITTING UP HERE TWIDDLING OUR THUMBS.

—Doris

355.
It's hard for me to
realize it's finished.

356. I won't know what to do if I'm not watching film or working on plays or worrying about one of my young men. I'll have to learn a whole lot of new ways.

357. I DON'T THINK I'LL BELIEVE HE WON'T BE BACK UNTIL I FINALLY SEE SOMEONE ELSE THERE NEXT YEAR. I DON'T THINK ANYONE REALLY BELIEVES THERE'LL BE A GRAMBLING TEAM WITHOUT COACH ROB.

    —*Pete Richardson, Southern University coach*

358. I'm going to quit to go where, to the doctor? I go to the doctor more than anybody I know. I don't have anything else to do.

359. I don't want a farewell tour. What is a farewell tour? People beat your brains out in a farewell tour.

360. A lot of people feel in their hearts that I don't know when it's time to step down. But it's hard for someone to make a decision for you when they don't know how you feel.

361. THE PHONES DON'T STOP RINGING, PEOPLE DON'T STOP COMING BY. IT'S A PIECE OF HISTORY THAT EVERYBODY WANTS TO BE IN ON.

> —*Scott Boatright, former Grambling State SID,*
> *on Eddie Robinson's final home game*

362. We always kid that whoever cries first is a sissy. And I'm always the sissy, because I always cry first, and this year I've cried often.

> —*on his final season*

363. If I had known all of this would disturb that many people, I would have never asked for another year.

364. YOU CAN'T THROW A GREAT COACH AND GENTLEMAN LIKE
     EDDIE ROBINSON OUT THE DOOR, NOT AFTER ALL HE HAS
     MEANT TO THE GAME.

     —*Bobby Bowden*

365. I don't feel that there will be any pressure in this final
     season. If I win them all this year, then I walk away
     smiling. And if I lose them all this year, I will still walk
     away. I won't like losing, but I can still walk away
     knowing that at least I had the opportunity to coach
     one more year.

366. I'm sure there are some people out there thinking that
     "Hey, Eddie Robinson has reached the age where he
     needs to step aside." Or they're thinking that Eddie is
     too old to get the job done anymore. The way our soci-
     ety is, the belief is that once a person gets to a certain
     age, they must retire.

367. Retire? Retire to what?

368. When I retire I'm going to work. I'm not going to sit home and wait on death like a lot of people. I'm not going to walk the streets saying, "I'm Eddie Robinson and I won football games."

369. I'll be back. (But) I don't control that. I'm going to recruit like I'm coming back, so we can whip somebody next year.

370. I stayed in quite a number of years, and I think we made the kind of contributions we wanted to make, did the things we wanted to do. I don't want to look back and say we stayed a little too long.

HIS LAST GAME

371. I'm really not trying to think of this game as my last. It's there in the back of my mind, but I'm really just trying to take this as just the next game we have to try and win.

372.
This is a day that I will never forget.

—after losing his final game of his fifty-seven-year career (Southern 30, Grambling State 7) on November 29, 1997

XI.
The Coach

The numbers tell the story.

Eddie Robinson, born on February 13, 1919, coached 588 college football games and won 408 of them. He has won more awards and been accorded more accolades than almost any other man in the coaching profession. Football games have been named in tribute to him, awards have been named in honor of him, books have been written to immortalize him, and museums are being erected to glorify him. He is a true legend in his own time.

He has challenged young people to be better tomorrow than they were today and to strive for excellence in everything they do. He has always been a fearless leader, an inspirational motivator, and a patient teacher.

Eddie Robinson is without a doubt the purest definition of the word "coach." Many will share the coaching moniker, but only a select few will ever truly embody the profession.

The winningest college football coach in America, with more than four hundred victories. (Grambling State University photo)

373. THEY CALL ME THE GREATEST. I KNOW THAT THE GREATEST
      FOOTBALL COACH WHO EVER STEPPED ONTO THE FIELD IS
      COACH EDDIE ROBINSON. I HAVE ADMIRED WHAT HE HAS
      DONE IN TURNING BOYS INTO MEN IN ADDITION TO BECOM-
      ING THE WINNINGEST COACH IN THE HISTORY OF THE GAME.
      HE IS A CREDIT TO HIS SPORT AS WELL AS A CREDIT TO
      HUMANITY.

      —*Muhammad Ali*

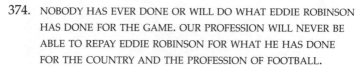

374. NOBODY HAS EVER DONE OR WILL DO WHAT EDDIE ROBINSON
      HAS DONE FOR THE GAME. OUR PROFESSION WILL NEVER BE
      ABLE TO REPAY EDDIE ROBINSON FOR WHAT HE HAS DONE
      FOR THE COUNTRY AND THE PROFESSION OF FOOTBALL.

      —*Joe Paterno*

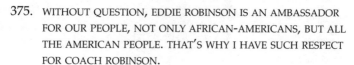

375. WITHOUT QUESTION, EDDIE ROBINSON IS AN AMBASSADOR
      FOR OUR PEOPLE, NOT ONLY AFRICAN-AMERICANS, BUT ALL
      THE AMERICAN PEOPLE. THAT'S WHY I HAVE SUCH RESPECT
      FOR COACH ROBINSON.

      —*Rev. Jesse Jackson*

376. COACH EDDIE ROBINSON'S NAME ALONE INVOKES IN ME IMMEDIATE THOUGHTS OF HIS CHARACTER, HIS WISDOM, HIS LOVE FOR STUDENT-ATHLETES, AND, OF COURSE, HIS WINNING. EDDIE ROBINSON IS THE EPITOME OF HUMANITY, COURAGE, AND PATRIOTISM.

—*Grant Teaff, former Baylor coach and executive director of the AFCA*

377. WORDS SIMPLY CANNOT EXPRESS HOW GRATEFUL AND HONORED I AM TO RECEIVE THE EDDIE ROBINSON AWARD. COACH ROBINSON IS ONE OF THE GREATEST GENTLEMEN OF THE GAME, AND TO RECEIVE THIS AWARD IN HIS NAME IS OVERWHELMING. I ACCEPT THIS GREAT AWARD ON BEHALF OF THE FOOTBALL TEAM AND COACHING STAFF HERE AT THE UNIVERSITY OF MONTANA.

—*Joe Glenn, after winning the 2000 Eddie Robinson (Coach of the Year) Award*

378. TO HEAR HIM STAND THERE AND TALK ABOUT HOW HUMBLE HE WAS TO BE HERE AT NOTRE DAME. I TOLD THEM . . . DON'T TAKE THIS FOR GRANTED. THEIR EYES WERE WIDE OPEN. IT GOT ME FIRED UP.

—*former Notre Dame coach Bob Davie, marveling after Robinson graced the Irish with his presence at a practice*

379. I'm a late crier. I cry late over good things.

380. LIKE A SOUTHERN BAPTIST PREACHER, EDDIE HAS EXTOLLED THE VIRTUES OF GOOD CITIZENSHIP, OBEYING YOUR PARENTS, RECEIVING A QUALITY EDUCATION, AND STAYING DRUG-FREE, TO YOUNG PEOPLE IN EVERY SPEECH HE DELIVERS, REGARDLESS OF THE SETTING.
    —*James Frank, Southwestern Athletic Conference commissioner*

381. I'm concerned about (Mike) Tyson. The young man needs help and I'm willing to counsel him.

382. THERE'S NO WAY IN THE WORLD THAT I COULD EVER REPAY HIM FOR WHAT HE'S MEANT TO ME.
    —*Ernie Ladd, former GSU and Kansas City Chiefs defensive lineman*

383. WHEN I GOT TO THE PROS, IT WAS EASY FOR ME BECAUSE OF
THE THINGS THAT I WENT THROUGH UNDER COACH ROBIN-
SON. HE MADE IT EASY FOR ME TO MAKE THE TRANSITION. A
CARPENTER CANNOT BUILD A HOUSE WITHOUT A SOLID
FOUNDATION. AN ATHLETE CANNOT PREPARE FOR THE NEXT
LEVEL WITHOUT THE PROPER NURTURING AND GUIDANCE
FROM HIS COACH.

—Willie Brown, NFL Hall of Fame cornerback

384. HE IS THE MOST INFLUENTIAL PERSON IN MY LIFE. HE'S THE
MOST UNIQUE PERSON THAT I HAVE EVER MET.

—Buck Buchanan, NFL Hall of Fame defensive lineman

385. HE WAS ALWAYS THERE WHEN I NEEDED HIM. THERE WERE
TIMES WHEN I WASN'T SURE IF PROFESSIONAL FOOTBALL WAS
FOR ME, BUT COACH ROBINSON ALWAYS ENCOURAGED ME TO
STICK WITH IT AND MAKE THE BEST OF IT.

—Charlie Joiner, NFL Hall of Fame receiver

386. I am going to talk loud, but I am not going to use pro-
fanity. When you here me say *damn* and *hell*, you have
heard it all.

387. WHEN I WAS WALKING ACROSS THE FIELD I FELT LIKE I HAD
      JUST COMPETED AGAINST MY DAD. IT WAS A DIFFERENT FEEL-
      ING, ONE THAT'S HARD TO DESCRIBE. IT WAS A WARM FEEL-
      ING OF EXUBERATION AND REGRET COMBINED.

      —*Houston Markham, former*
      Alabama State coach and Alcorn State player

388. A lot is expected from whom a lot is given.

389. I don't know that I've given as much as I've received.

390. HE'S TRULY ONE OF THE LEGENDS OF COLLEGE FOOTBALL
      AND IS A CREDIT TO THE PROFESSION AND THE SPORT.
      —*W. C. Gordon, former Jackson State University head coach*

391. EDDIE ROBINSON IS A NATURAL CHOICE FOR THIS FIRST
      AWARD. HE HAS EXEMPLIFIED THROUGH FIFTY YEARS IN
      COLLEGE FOOTBALL WHAT A TREMENDOUS INFLUENCE A
      COACH CAN HAVE ON HIS PLAYERS, PAST AND PRESENT.

      —*Don Anderson, executive director of the Orange*
      County Sports Association, on Robinson's being named
      the first recipient of the College Football Heritage Award

392. HE'S A TRUE LIVING LEGEND. WE DON'T HAVE TOO MANY OF
     THEM, PERIOD, AND WE DON'T HAVE ANY BLACK LEGENDS.
                                                —*Houston Markham*

393. I REMEMBER ONE YEAR, A FRESHMAN PLAYER ON THE TEAM
     FORGOT TO WEAR A TIE WHEN HE GOT ON THE BUS. WHEN I
     SAW HIM, I SAID, "OH NO, HE'LL NEVER MAKE THIS TRIP.
     COACH ROBINSON IS GOING TO CHEW HIM OUT." THE NEXT
     TIME WE WENT ON A ROAD TRIP, THAT PLAYER WAS DRESSED
     SHARPER THAN CALVIN KLEIN.
                                                  —*Doug Williams*

394. I just try to stick with what I know and what I like to
     do. I try not to profess to something I'm not.

395. HE'S A HERO IN THAT HE'S SET THE PACE IN COLLEGE FOOT-
     BALL. ONE, BY THE NUMBER OF WINS. TWO, BY THE WAY HE
     TREATS HIS BOYS. AND HE'S A GENTLEMAN, NOT JUST TO
     GRAMBLING, BUT HE'S BEEN AN AMBASSADOR TO ALL THE
     SCHOOLS IN THE SOUTHWESTERN ATHLETIC CONFERENCE.
                                    —*Lee Hardman, Arkansas-Pine Bluff coach*

396. NOBODY CAN FOLLOW IN HIS FOOTSTEPS. THOSE SHOES ARE TOO BIG TO FILL. HE'S NOT ONLY A GREAT COACH, BUT HE IS A GREAT MAN. THAT'S WHAT MAKES HIM SO SPECIAL. THAT'S WHY HE IS EMBRACED ALL OVER THE WORLD. THERE WILL NEVER BE ANOTHER ONE LIKE HIM. PERIOD.

—Doug Williams

397. COACH ROBINSON'S ACTIONS ON AND OFF THE FIELD INDICATE IN EVERY WAY THAT THIS MAN IS A LEGEND.

—Jon F. Hanson, chairman of the National Football Foundation

398. THE GUY'S A LEGEND IN HIS CONTRIBUTIONS TO AMERICA, NOT JUST GRAMBLING. HE'S A FOLK HERO AND DESERVES TO BE ON A STAMP.

—Houston Markham

399. HE HAD A TREMENDOUS INFLUENCE ON MY LIFE. HE WAS LIKE A FATHER TO ME. WITHOUT EDDIE, SO MANY OF THE GOOD THINGS IN MY LIFE WOULD HAVE NEVER BEEN POSSIBLE.

—Paul "Tank" Younger, former Grambling State star

400. This means a lot to me because a lot of people involved are people I grew up with in the Baton Rouge area. This is truly a great moment for us. Growing up, I always thought I'd go to Southern but ended up at nearby Leland. It's hard to believe that after all this time, I'm getting a degree from Southern. It's something I'll always honor and treasure.

—on his honorary doctorate of
human letters from arch rival Southern

401. WHAT HE TAUGHT ME WHEN I PLAYED FOR HIM CARRIED OVER LATER INTO MY LIFE. IT WASN'T JUST HIS FOOTBALL PHILOSOPHY, IT WAS HIS PHILOSOPHY ABOUT LIFE.

—Ernie Ladd

402. A lot has been given to Eddie Robinson, and I always felt that it's fitting to give something back, so that's what we tried to do in our profession. It's a profession of love . . . and I feel that I could crank it up and go another fifty years and get it right.

403.   WE NEVER FELT COACH WAS NOT BEING HONEST WITH US
       WHEN HE CRIED. ONCE YOU GET TO KNOW HIM AS PLAYERS,
       YOU REALIZE THAT HE GETS SO WRAPPED UP IN THE EMOTION
       OF THE GAME THAT HE HAS TO CRY. MANY OF US REACHED
       SUCH AN EMOTIONAL LEVEL THAT WE WERE CRYING WITH HIM.
                                              —*Doug Williams*

404.   You've got to believe in what you are doing as a teacher,
       coach, minister, or businessman. I consider myself as
       having adopted traits from each of these professions.

405.   HIS NAME IS LINKED NATIONALLY TO NOT ONLY BLACK
       COLLEGE SPORTS, BUT SPORTS IN GENERAL.
                              —*Warren Jacobsen, ABC Radio host*

406.   EDDIE ROBINSON IS AN ICON. HE IS AN ICON FOR BLACK
       COLLEGE FOOTBALL.
                    —*Larry Little, former North Carolina Central coach*

407.   HE IS IN ANOTHER ZONE. I DON'T KNOW IF WE'LL EVER SEE
       THOSE DAYS ANYMORE. EVER.
                                              —*Bobby Bowden*

408.

THERE WILL NEVER BE ANOTHER COACH LIKE EDDIE ROBINSON.

—*Ernie Ladd*

NOTES

I. The Game

1. Eddie Robinson remarks at 1990 AFCA convention.
2. Grambling State University press release.
3. Ibid.
4. *Shreveport Times*, October 10, 1997.
5. O. K. Davis, *Ruston Daily Leader*.
6. Ibid.
7. *The Sporting News*, December 12, 1994.
8. Grambling State University press release.
9. Yancey Roy, *Lake Charles (La.) Press*, August 1, 1990.
10. Ibid.
11. Associated Press.
12. Author's notes.
13. Ibid.
14. Eddie Robinson remarks at 1990 AFCA convention.
15. Grambling State University press release.
16. *The Sporting News*, December 12, 1994.
17. Grambling State University press release.
18. Marty Mule, publication unknown.
19. Author's notes.
20. Grambling State University press release.
21. O. K. Davis, *Ruston Daily Leader*.
22. Southwestern Athletic Conference press release.
23. Ibid.
24. O. K. Davis, *Ruston Daily Leader*.
25. Ibid.
26. Ibid.
27. Ibid.
28. Ibid.
29. Ibid.
30. Ibid.
31. Ibid.

II. The Job

32. Grambling State University press release.
33. *The Sporting News*, December 12, 1994.
34. Grambling State University press release.
35. *Jet*, September 2, 1985.
36. Walter Leavy, *Ebony*, December 1985.
37. Ibid.
38. *The Sporting News*, December 12, 1994.
39. Eddie Robinson remarks at 1990 AFCA convention.
40. Ibid.
41. O. K. Davis, *Football Digest*, April 1993.
42. *The Sporting News*, December 12, 1994.
43. Ibid.
44. Ibid.
45. Ibid.
46. Bill Bryant, *Birmingham News*.
47. Reggie Benson, *Shreveport Times*.
48. Ibid.
49. Grambling State University press release.
50. Bob Stockard, *Black Collegian*, April 1996.
51. Richard Lapchick, *The Sporting News*.
52. Grambling State University press release.
53. *Detroit Free Press*, September 6, 1990.
54. Grambling State University press release.
55. Michael Wallace, *Gramblinite*.
56. Roger B. Brown, *Fort Worth Star-Telegram*.
57. Mary Foster, *Shreveport Times*, December 13, 1996.
58. O. K. Davis, *Ruston Daily Leader*.
59. Adler, Larry, *Football Coach Quotes: The Wit, Wisdom and Winning Words of Leaders on the Gridiron*. Jefferson, NC: McFarland & Company, 1992.

60. Freeman, Criswell, *The Wisdom of Southern Football: Common Sense and Uncommon Genius from 101 Gridiron Greats*. Nashville, TN: Walnut Grove Press, 1995.
61. Walter Leavy, *Ebony*, December 1985.
62. *The Sporting News*, December 12, 1994.
63. Eddie Robinson remarks at 1990 AFCA convention.
64. O. K. Davis, *Football Digest*, April 1993.
65. Ibid.
66. Ibid.
67. Ibid.
68. Author's notes.
69. *Detroit Free Press*.
70. Eddie Robinson remarks at 1990 AFCA convention.
71. Ibid.
72. Ibid.
73. Ibid.
74. Ibid.
75. Ibid.
76. Ibid.
77. O. K. Davis, *Football Digest*, April 1993.
78. Sam King, *Baton Rouge Advocate*.
79. Ibid.
80. Ibid.
81. Ibid.

III. The Victories

82. Grambling State University media guide, 1997.
83. Grambling State University press release.
84. Eddie Robinson remarks at 1990 AFCA convention.
85. Ibid.
86. Ibid.
87. *The Sporting News*, December 12, 1994.
88. Ibid.
89. Ibid.
90. Ibid.
91. Yancey Roy, *Lake Charles American Press*, August 1, 1990.
92. Reggie Benson, *Shreveport Times*.
93. Jenna Halvatgis, Associated Press.
94. Robinson, Eddie, with Richard Lapchick, *Never Before, Never Again*. New York: St. Martin's Press, 1999.
95. Ibid.
96. Curtis Heyen, *Shreveport Times*.
97. Grambling State University press release.
98. Ibid.
99. Mary Foster, *Shreveport Times*.
100. O. K. Davis, *Ruston Daily Leader*, December 11, 1996.
101. Ibid.
102. Ibid.
103. Freeman, Criswell, *The Wisdom of Southern Football: Common Sense and Uncommon Genius from 101 Gridiron Greats*.
104. Jerome Brondfield, *Reader's Digest*, September 1986.
105. Sam King, *Baton Rouge Advocate*.

IV. The Losses

106. Grambling State University media guide, 1997.
107. O. K. Davis, *Ruston Daily Leader*.
108. Bill Bryant, *Birmingham News*.
109. O. K. Davis, *Ruston Daily Leader*.
110. Bill Bryant, *Birmingham News*.
111. Grambling State University press release.
112. Yancey Roy, *Lake Charles American Press*, August 1, 1990.
113. Reggie Benson, *Shreveport Times*.
114. Ibid.
115. Grambling State University press release.
116. Ibid.
117. Robinson and Lapchick, *Never Before, Never Again*.
118. Ibid.

119. O. K. Davis, *Ruston Daily Leader*.
120. Grambling State University press release.
121. *Detroit Free Press*, February 1, 1988.
122. John Marcase, publication unknown.
123. Ibid.
124. Brian Eastman, *Shreveport Times*, November 16, 1997.
125. Ibid.
126. Thomas Murphy, *News Star*, December 10, 1996.
127. Ibid.
128. Fred Robinson, *Times-Picayune*, November 28, 1996.
129. O. K. Davis, *Ruston Daily Leader*.
130. *Shreveport Times*, November 16, 1997.
131. Ibid.
132. Ibid.
133. Thomas Murphy, *News Star*.
134. Bill Campbell, *Times-Picayune*, December 11, 1997.
135. *Baton Rouge Advocate*.
136. Ibid.
137. Ibid.
138. *Baton Rouge Advocate*.
139. O K. Davis, *Ruston Daily Leader*, December 11, 1996.
140. Adler, *Football Coach Quotes: The Wit, Wisdom and Winning Words of Leaders on the Gridiron*.

V. The Record

141. Grambling State University media guide, 1997.
142. Ibid.
143. Southwestern Athletic Conference press release.
144. Walter Leavy, *Ebony*, December 1985.
145. Grambling State University media guide, 1997.
146. Ibid.
147. Southwestern Athletic Conference press release.
148. Ibid.
149. *The Sporting News*, December 12, 1994.
150. Ibid.
151. Ibid.
152. Ibid.
153. Ibid.
154. Yancey Roy, *Lake Charles American Press*, August 1, 1990.
155. O. K. Davis, *Ruston Daily Leader*.
156. Bill McIntyre, *Shreveport Times*.
157. Ibid.
158. Ibid.
159. Ibid.
160. Neal Farmer, *Houston Chronicle*.
161. Grambling State University press release.
162. Ibid.
163. Robinson and Lapchick, *Never Before, Never Again*.
164. *Sports Illustrated*, October 14, 1985.
165. Tom D'Angelo, *Palm Beach Post*, August 24, 2002.
166. Grambling State University press release.
167. Associated Press.
168. *Baton Rouge Advocate*.
169. Grambling State University press release.
170. Associated Press.
171. Neal Farmer, *Houston Chronicle*.
172. bid.
173. Bill Bryant, *Birmingham News*.
174. Neal Farmer, *Houston Chronicle*.
175. Ibid.
176. Ibid.
177. Jenna Halvatgis, Associated Press.
178. Ibid.
179. Neal Farmer, *Houston Chronicle*.
180. Ibid.
181. Ibid.

VI. The School

182. *Jet*, September 2, 1985.
183. Grambling State University press release.
184. Grambling State University media guide, 1997.
185. Ibid.
186. Grambling State University press release.
187. Southwestern Athletic Conference press release.
188. Ibid.
189. *The Sporting News*, December 12, 1994.
190. Jim McLain, *Shreveport Times*.
191. Ibid.
192. John Deshazier, *Times-Picayune*.
193. Grambling State University press release.
194. Ibid.
195. Ibid.
196. O. K. Davis, *Black Collegian*, November/December 1990.
197. Ibid.
198. Ibid.
199. Thomas Murphy, *News Star*, December 10, 1996.
200. O. K. Davis, *Ruston Daily Leader*, September 27, 1982.
201. *The Sporting News*, December 12, 1994.
202. Ibid.
203. Tom Weir, *USA Today*.
204. O. K. Davis, *Ruston Daily Leader*.
205. Ibid.
206. Adler, *Football Coach Quotes: The Wit, Wisdom and Winning Words of Leaders on the Gridiron*.
207. Ibid.
208. Grambling State University press release.
209. Grambling State University, media guide, 1997.
210. O. K. Davis, *Football Digest*, April 1993.
211. Ibid.
212. Grambling State University press release.
213. Ibid.
214. Ibid.
215. Ibid.
216. O. K. Davis, *Black Collegian*, November/December 1990.
217. Tom Weir, *USA Today*.
218. Bob Stockard, *Black Collegian*, April 1996.
219. Ibid.
220. Ibid.
221. Jerome Brondfield, *Reader's Digest*, September 1986.
222. Eddie Robinson remarks at 1990 AFCA convention.
223. Ibid.
224. Ibid.
225. Ibid.

VII. The Players

226. Adler, *Football Coach Quotes: The Wit, Wisdom and Winning Words of Leaders on the Gridiron*.
227. Grambling State University press release.
228. O. K. Davis, *Ruston Daily Leader*.
229. Eddie Robinson, remarks at 1990 AFCA convention.
230. Ibid.
231. *The Sporting News*, December 12, 1994.
232. Ibid.
233. Ibid.
234. Ibid.
235. Ibid.
236. Ibid.
237. Ibid.
238. Ibid.
239. Ibid.
240. Ibid.
241. Ibid.
242. Ibid.
243. Ibid.
244. Ibid.

245. Ibid.

246. Ibid.

247. Neal Farmer, *Houston Chronicle*.

248. Ibid.

249. Grambling State University press release.

250. Ibid.

251. Ibid.

252. Ibid.

253. O. K. Davis, *Black Collegian*, November/December 1990.

254. Ibid.

255. Grambling State University press release.

256. O. K. Davis, *Black Collegian*, November/December 1990.

257. Davis, O. K. *Grambling's Gridiron Glory: Eddie Robinson and the Tigers' Success Story*. Ruston, LA... M & M Printing Company, 1983.

258. Bob Stockard, *Black Collegian*, April 1996.

259. Adler, *Football Coach Quotes: The Wit, Wisdom and Winning Words of Leaders on the Gridiron*.

260. Bob Stockard, *Black Collegian*, April 1996.

261. Freeman, *The Wisdom of Southern Football: Common Sense and Uncommon Genius from 101 Gridiron Greats*.

262. Ibid.

263. Ibid.

264. Author's notes.

265. Sam King, *Baton Rouge Advocate*.

266. Andy Furman, *Scholastic Roundup*.

267. Grambling State University press release.

268. Ibid.

269. Eddie Robinson remarks at 1990 AFCA convention.

270. Grambling State University press release.

271. Author's notes.

272. Grambling State University press release.

273. Associated Press.

274. Ibid.

275. Eddie Robinson, remarks at 1990 AFCA convention.

276. Ibid.

277. Ibid.

278. Author's notes.

279. Ibid.

280. Ibid.

281. Eddie Robinson remarks at 1990 AFCA convention.

282. Author's notes.

283. Ibid.

VIII. The Family

284. O. K. Davis, *Football Digest*, April 1993.

285. Southwestern Athletic Conference press release.

286. Ibid.

287. Grambling State University press release.

288. *The Sporting News*, December 12, 1994.

289. Ibid.

290. Ibid.

291. Mary Foster, *Shreveport Times*, July 10, 1998.

292. Jerome Brondfield, *Reader's Digest*, September 1986.

293. O. K. Davis, *Ruston Daily Leader*.

294. Ibid.

295. Ibid.

296. Grambling State University press release.

297. *The Sporting News*, December 12, 1994.

298. Jenna Halvatgis, Associated Press.

299. O. K. Davis, *Ruston Daily Leader*, December 15, 1996.

300. *Baton Rouge Advocate*.

301. O. K. Davis, *Football Digest*, April 1993.

302. Ibid.

303. Mary Foster, *Shreveport Times*.

304. Grambling State University sports information.

305. *Reflections of a Champion.* Dallas: Box Square Entertainment, Inc., 1997.

306. Grambling State University media guide, 1997.

307. Craig Lenniger, publication unknown.

308. Ibid.

309. Ibid.

310. Ibid.

311. O. K. Davis, *Ruston Daily Leader.*

312. *Detroit Free Press.*

313. Ibid.

314. Jerome Brondfield, *Reader's Digest,* September 1986.

IX. The Country

315. Grambling State University press release.

316. Mary Foster, Associated Press.

317. Mary Margaret Van Diest, February 9, 2001, publication unknown.

318. Ibid.

319. Ibid.

320. Grambling State University press release.

321. Ibid.

322. Ibid.

323. Ibid.

324. Grambling State University,media guide, 1997.

325. Eddie Robinson remarks at 1990 AFCA convention.

326. Southwestern Athletic Conference press release.

327. *The Sporting News,* December 12, 1994.

328. Grambling State University press release.

329. Robinson and Lapchick, *Never Before, Never Again.*

330. Grambling State University press release.

331. O. K. Davis, *Ruston Daily Leader,* September 27, 1982.

332. Tom Weir, Gannett News Service.

333. Adler, *Football Coach Quotes: The Wit, Wisdom and Winning Words of Leaders on the Gridiron.*

334. Ibid.

335. Freeman, *The Wisdom of Southern Football: Common Sense and Uncommon Genius from 101 Gridiron Greats.*

336. Author's notes.

337. Kimberly Whitfield, *Gramblinite,* December 2001.

338. Ibid.

339. Grambling State University press release.

340. Walter Leavy, *Ebony,* December 1985.

341. O. K. Davis, *Ruston Daily Leader.*

342. *Detroit Free Press,* September 6, 1990.

343. *Sports Illustrated,* October 14, 1985.

344. Ibid.

345. *The Sporting News,* December 12, 1994.

346. Adler, *Football Coach Quotes: The Wit, Wisdom and Winning Words of Leaders on the Gridiron.*

X. The End

347. Grambling State University press release.

348. John Hill and Thomas Murphy, *News Star.*

349. Michael Wallace, *Gramblinite.*

350. O. K. Davis, *Ruston Daily Leader.*

351. Ibid.

352. Mary Foster, *Shreveport Times.*

353. Ibid.

354. Ibid.

355. *Shreveport Times,* November 29, 1997.

356. Ibid.

357. Ibid.

358. Fred Robinson, *Times-Picayune,* November 28, 1996.

359. Bill Campbell, *Times-Picayune,* December 11, 1997.

360. Ibid.

361. *Shreveport Times*.
362. Ibid.
363. O. K. Davis, *Ruston Daily Leader*, December 15, 1996.
364. Ibid.
365. Ibid.
366. Ibid., December 11, 1996.
367. Mary Foster, *Shreveport Times*, July 10, 1998.
368. Michelle Landry, *Gramblinite*.
369. Tom Murphy, *News Star*.
370. Tom D'Angelo, *Palm Beach Post*, August 24, 2002.
371. Jim McLain, *Shreveport Times*.
372. Mary Foster, Associated Press.

XI. The Coach

373. Robinson and Lapchick, *Never Before, Never Again*.
374. Ibid.
375. Ibid.
376. Ibid.
377. Associated Press.
378. David Haugh, publication unknown.
379. Southwestern Athletic Conference press release.
380. Ibid.
381. Ibid.
382. O. K. Davis, *Football Digest*, April 1993.
383. Ibid.
384. Ibid.
385. Ibid.
386. *The Sporting News*, December 12, 1994.
387. Bill Bryant, *Birmingham News*.
388. Yancey Roy, *Lake Charles American Press*, August 1, 1990.
389. Ibid.
390. O. K. Davis, *Ruston Daily Leader*.
391. Orange County Sports Association, July 10, 1990.
392. Larry Gross, publication unknown.
393. O. K. Davis, *Black Collegian*, November/December 1990.
394. O. K. Davis, *Ruston Daily Leader*, September 27, 1982.
395. Adam Rubin, *Shreveport Times*.
396. Roger B. Brown, *Fort Worth Star-Telegram*.
397. *Baton Rouge Advocate*, September 28, 1997.
398. Associated Press.
399. O. K. Davis, *Ruston Daily Leader*, March 1, 1993.
400. *Shreveport Times*, May 7, 1998.
401. O. K. Davis, *Ruston Daily Leader*.
402. Associated Press.
403. Bob Stockard, *Black Collegian*, April 1996.
404. Ibid.
405. O. K. Davis, *Ruston Daily Leader*.
406. Author's notes.
407. Tom D'Angelo, *Palm Beach Post*, August 24, 2002.
408. O. K. Davis, *Ruston Daily Leader*.